Hoof to Heart

...a guide to understanding grief, loss and the healing power of the horse

KIMBERLY K. HENRY, MS, CTS, CT

Printed in the United States, May 2008.

13-digit ISBN: 978-0-6152-1288-3

Hoof to Heart

...a guide to understanding grief, loss and the healing power of the horse

KIMBERLY K. HENRY, MS, CTS, CT

Jacket photographs: Lori Bell, Clear as a Bell Photography

Inside photographs: Lauren Dukes, Lori Bell & Adrienne R. Schwarte

Book & jacket design: Adrienne R. Schwarte

Calvin and Kim Henry

Kim Henry holds a Masters in Therapeutic Recreation and a Masters in Inclusive Early Childhood Special Education, encompassing 15 years focused on hospice work, the grief and loss issues of children, teens and families and providing community education relating to loss.

She is certified through EAGALA (Equine Assisted Growth and Learning Association), while also being a Certified Bereavement Facilitator/Specialist with the American Academy of Bereavement, a member of the Association of Death, Education and Counseling where she is certified as a Thanatologist (grief counselor) and has completed her certification as a Trauma Specialist through The National Institute for Trauma and Loss in Children.

She is the founder and executive director of Mane Support, Inc., a non-profit organization that provides an equine assisted grief counseling ministry for children, youth, teens, adults and families. More information about Mane Support can be found at **www.manesupport.org.**

Contents

‹introduction›

The inevitable truth for all of mankind is that we all will experience loss and pain in our life. If we have the privilege of being chosen to work with those who are hurting, then we have been truly blessed. If we open our hearts and minds to using the horse as our companion and really hear their voice, then we have been granted more blessings than one human can hope for.

This book is designed to be a guide for those who counsel children and adults, as it is a shared compilation of many thoughts, experiences and knowledge that I have had the privilege of learning from others, both participants and professionals, and from the horses. I would like to first strongly encourage you to continue to learn by reading and studying theories and definitions of the field, as they are continually changing. Secondly, I would like to suggest that you take care of yourself as you travel this journey of healing. By taking care of yourself first you will be able to endure the road you have been given to travel and by opening up yourself to learning you will never be alone.

My journey began as an accident...or so I thought. After about 12 years in hospice work, it seemed natural to focus on the needs of children and provide them with an avenue all their own. A colleague and friend shared in this vision and so we opened KICS, Kids In Crisis Support, Inc. A nonprofit designed to meet the needs of children and teens who were grieving. Things were moving as they do with any nonprofit...you have your challenges...but it was going well. After many days of hearing the stories of these children, I began to realize that I needed an outlet...a place to clear my head and process my own reactions to their stories. In this longing for a quiet space to call my own, I found myself drawn to a love of my childhood, the horse. As if opening your window on a crisp, clear Spring morning, just being around the horses gave me air. It was the air that I so desperately needed to focus on the real world, the day to day reality of grief and loss. One thing lead to another and with my husband by my side, we bought what I like to call my "mid-life crisis", Two-T Yankee Gold. – Yank for short. I sought out the only organization that I knew that would allow me to join the horse with grief counseling and thus allow me to share this avenue of healing with the families that we work with, EAGALA (Equine Assisted Growth and Learning Association). After receiving my first certification from EAGALA, Mane Support was born under KICS. To EAGALA, I will be eternally grateful for this opportunity.

The next year I had the honor of presenting at an EAGALA conference, and here another vision became crystal clear. What had already begun as a program under KICS, needed to jump on its own horse and ride, if you will. And so Mane Support was separated from KICS and became its own nonprofit in November of 2006. We serve children, teens, families and individuals who have experienced a death, who are anticipating the death of someone they know, or who have experienced other types of trauma.

So do I still think that what happened in such a short period of time was an accident? Let's just say that I feel that the Lord has entrusted me with one of the greatest jobs of my life and has given me the privilege of working with one of His greatest creatures...the horse. For this gift, I am truly humbled and eternally grateful to Him.

I would like to dedicate this book to my husband Calvin, who has an incredible tolerance for my ideas, while loving and supporting me through it all. His faith, integrity and views on life hold me up, when I find it difficult to stand on my own. To my friends who are still my friends, even when my return phone calls and conversations are few and far between. To my horse Yank, and other equine friends, who teach me more about myself and the value of each moment of the day. And to the wonderful memories of my mom, dad, brother and dear friend Lora Ward, who taught me how to have faith, live and enjoy life, in so many ways.

I hope that this guide is helpful....enjoy your blessings!!!

<chapter one>

Understanding Yourself, Understanding Grief, Mourning and Bereavement

In working with children, youth, adults and/or families who are grieving it is important that first you understand your own aversions, memories and experiences with grief. It is all a part of taking care of yourself. Something that so many of us in the helping professions tend to put aside.

Take time to review and remember the losses that you have experienced in your life. The thoughts and feelings that could surface might surprise you, but better to be surprised on your own terms than in the middle of a session with a participant. By engaging in this type of self reflection, will this ensure that you will never experience the "triggers" of your own personal grief as you listen to the stories and experiences of others? I wish that I could answer "yes" to that question but that would only contradict the discussion and realizations regarding the grieving process and the work that we do. Remember that the "grieving process" is just what it says it is...*it is a process not an event.* Learning to incorporate the losses into one's life rather than disregarding their significance and impact, is one of the greatest tools you can obtain. So with that in mind remember to allow yourself the opportunities that you need to heal as you travel with others on this life long, life changing process and journey. Find your own outlets, like the ones that you recommend to those you work with, and **USE THEM**. Talking about taking care of yourself and your needs is wonderful lip service but does not gain any ground for you. I once had someone tell me that I was a "sponge" when it came to counseling others. Can you believe for a time I took that as a compliment? Then I began to think about the sponge. When you saturate it with water it either holds

as much as it can until it begins to drip uncontrollably, it mildews or it shrivels up and dies. Now I ask you...are any these attributes appealing to you? If you are working in or have an interest in the field of equine assisted psychotherapy, EAP, then you have no better teacher than the horse to assist you in recognizing the intricacies that define you as a person. Listen to them as they do you. But be prepared, they tend to be more honest with us than we can be with ourselves. We will learn more about the Equine Counselor in Chapter 6.

Also become familiar with your own personal "linking objects." These are usually tangible objects that represent the person who died. For instance, a piece of jewelry or an article of clothing. They can actually *link* us back to that person in some way or another. This will also be a good piece of information to have when working with others, as sometimes these linking objects can also be triggers in their grief. Having insight into the concepts of linking objects and triggers will allow you to further understand the connections that are still there for those you are working with and for yourself.

As important as it is to be able to recognize your own grief and limitations, (yes that was the word limitations), it is also a good idea to know the differences between some of the words/terms that are used in the field of thanantology (death and dying). Often times they serve as the reminders we need to put things back into perspective, be able to really hear the hidden thoughts of the participants or give us an emotional timeline. For myself there are four main ones: Anticipatory Grief, Grief, Mourning, and Bereavement. Simply stated they can be defined as follows, keeping in mind that research and actual definitions are more inclusive.

Anticipatory Grief
The emotions, thoughts and feelings of grief that is processed and experienced in anticipation of a death. My personal opinion is that anticipatory grief can be experienced by both the caregiver and the person who is dying. It is a process of changing and accepting with many areas of debate in between.

Grief
The reaction to the death, which takes place in thoughts and feelings as well as the physical, behavioral, spiritual and emotional responses.

Mourning
The active part of grieving, ranging from rituals to physical outward expressions. It is closely related to grief but it's not so much the reaction to loss but the process in which the person integrates the death into their life.

Bereavement
Used to describe the situation following a death. If someone has experienced a death then they are said to be bereaved.

Other terms that you might hear, recognize and would be of a great advantage to learn about are Complicated Grief and Disenfranchised Grief.

Complicated Grief is just what it says; a complication caused unresolved grief related issues. Because grief is so very multifaceted, these issues could be pertaining to circumstances before the death, or a pyramid of occurrences following. Thereby rendering the person who is grieving, "stuck" in their ability to begin to heal. This type of experience obviously intensifies the grieving process and can leave behind a path of emotional numbness and mental/physical destruction.

Disenfranchised Grief is best defined by Ken Doka. In his book, *Disenfranchised Grief: Recognizing Hidden Sorrow,* he defines this grief type as "grief that persons experience when they incur a loss that is not or cannot be openly acknowledged, socially sanctioned or publicly mourned." (p.4) Understanding that there are many different norms for different societies, can you imagine not be able to grieve the loss of someone you love because it is not acceptable to do so? The emotional, psychological, spiritual and physical effects are tremendous. Several examples of disenfranchised grievers are families or friends of those who have completed suicide, children who are viewed as too young to grieve or families and friends of those who die with AIDS. The list can go on and on as you explore different cultures, beliefs and family systems. I again strongly encourage you to read the work of Ken Doka and others, to further your knowledge in this area. The correlations that are made are extremely helpful in working with those who are grieving.

Another area worthy of mentioning and one that you will want to explore is that of Acute Grief Response, its meaning, phases and manifestations. This type of response is related to the experience of the death and can manifest itself in many physical, emotional, social and behavioral symptoms. Often diagnosed by a therapist or physician, Acute Grief Response can present warning signs that are closely related to that of a medical emergency. For example, tightness in the throat or chest, lack of strength, abdominal pain, withdrawn, hyperactive, hallucinations of the person who has died (visual or auditory) and preoccupation of one's own death.

<11>

chapter one

Having increased knowledge and awareness of these types of responses will provide you with better identification and differentiating skills.

Take time to become familiar with these terms and any others that are pertinent to the work that you are doing. It will provide you with a broader foundational understanding, while giving the participants the full benefit of the support they deserve from the knowledge that you have.

In addition to "terms" there are also "types" of loss, other than death. Whether subtle or obvious to you, it is important to never underestimate the roles they may play in one's life. Examples of types of loss are:

- Death of a spouse
- Death of a partner
- Death of a parent
- Death of a child
- Death of a sibling
- Death of another relative
- Death of a classmate and/or colleague
- Death of a pet
- Serious illness of a loved one
- Loss of ones own health through an illness
- Loss of financial stability resulting from a death of a spouse and/or family member
- Moving to a new neighborhood

....and the list goes on.

Recognizing your own acceptance and aversions to the types of loss you have experienced, will also better prepare you to hear the stories of others, as you continue to take care of yourself.

Guilt, blame and shame are also a part of understanding an individual's grief and loss issues. These will be discussed further in Chapter Four, relating to adults. But whether a child or an adult, survivor's guilt can complicate and stifle the healing process. This is another aspect of grieving to become familiar with. By doing so you will be able to assist the participant in the development of coping skills, that can facilitate a pathway of restoration for their life.

Lastly, as you become more comfortable with you own grief and loss, terms, types, etc. and begin to reach out to others who are hurting; there are some suggested ways that you can be of support. As you may be aware, when you are grieving there are many thoughts and feelings that can surface and vacillate, on a daily if not hourly basis. Differentiate between yours and theirs and try initiating any one of the following:

- Just sit with the person and be there.

- Allow people to be sad.

- Really listen, not just hear, what they have to say.

- Give them time to tell their story over and over again.

- Acknowledge and validate the pain that they are feeling.

- Carefully share your thoughts and feelings about your own loss.

- Make telephone calls, run errands or send a card.

‹chapter two›

Grief and Trauma. . .
Is there really a difference?

N
ow that you have a better understanding of the definitions of grief, loss and bereavement to work with, let's throw in trauma. Trauma is composed of grief reactions in diverse facets. A person can experience individualized manners of grieving without being traumatized by a situation or event, but rarely is the opposite true. From a personal perspective, trauma is something that I do not take lightly. I would like to caution those of you who are considering working with

those who have experienced life changing traumatic events. Read, learn and consult with other professionals in the field to understand all that you can about trauma, prior to entering into this work. It can be an unsettled place for participants to be and their existence can be enmeshed into their experience, thereby rendering them helpless to unfreeze their responses. As it can be in various counseling environments, some well meaning assistance can be more detrimental in the long run. The following information is a brief outline to peak your interest; the rest is up to you.

Is there really a difference between grief and trauma? The National Institute for Trauma and Loss in Children gives very clear and concise differences between the two. These are not all inclusive, but definitely provide an outline for a beginning into understanding what differentiates between the two. They are as follows:

Grief
General reaction is sadness
Does not disfigure personal identity
Dreams tend to be about the person who died
Personal guilt states, *"I wish I would/would not have"*

Trauma
General reaction is terror
Attacks and disfigures identity
Dreams are about the child dying or being hurt
Personal guilt states, *"It was my fault, I could have prevented it"*

If you are working with individuals whose grief is defined by trauma, time and safety are very important factors. Take time to understand the fight, flight or freeze responses. If your work incorporates the horse, take time to understand their coinciding responses and cross reference them. For instance, have you ever watched a horse whose keen sense of smell has been triggered by something burning in the distance? An odor that we cannot even begin to detect with our abilities. They stop, ears up, nostrils flared and freeze. Eventually their natural instinct will kick in and they will either take the "flight" approach and leave their perceived danger immediately or they will reconcile safety within their mind and resume their activity. Compare that now to an individual who has experienced a traumatic event. Their senses of that occurrence are heightened just as that of the horse. The difference between the two now lies in the way that the information or input is being processed in the brain. Instead of the "flight" or even the "fight" response, there is now the "freeze". Just as the children that we will talk about in Chapter 3 are sometimes "stuck" at a particular developmental level when a death has occurred, so these individuals are also stuck or frozen at a crucial point, within their trama experience. To create movement; which can eventually create healing; it is important that you be able to be a witness to their story. Just as the horse lives in the moment, so you too must live in that moment with this participant. This is where you find out how important it was and is that you educate yourself into the intricacies of trauma. Call on your resources that you have developed to assist you in understanding the tools to use when you are hearing the occurrences that has trapped this individual.

Within their story there will also be Psychological and Emotional symptoms/reactions that will give further insight into their story. An example of these, are as follows:

Psychological
>Shock, leading to terror
>Hypervigalance
>Self-blame and self-hatred
>A disconnect with self and others

Emotional

      Heightened panic

      Extreme fear

      Anger

      Worry

      Isolating from others

As with grief reactions, physical symptoms or reactions such as body aches, visualizations of the event, fatigue or hyperactivity could be seen. In addition there could also be spiritual symptoms or reactions such as disbelief or difficulty in an organized institution to indulgence into a specific faith, religion or leader. As individual as we are, so are the symptoms and reactions to grief and trauma. By being observant, just as you are with the horses, of physical, emotional and behavioral responses, you will be able to obtain information into the event, the perception of the event and the processing taking place.

Whatever the situation, understanding that our past makes up part of who we are and our future outlook gives us places to go, rely on one of the key attributes of equine behavior when working with grief or trauma...live in the moment.

<chapter three>

Looking at Loss Through the Eyes of a Child

F or those of you who work with children or who have children of your own, you have been introduced to an incredible world of understanding, creative thinking and honesty.

When we talk about children and grief, there is a statement that I seem to hear often. Children are so resilient...he or she will bounce right back from this death. To this and other assumptions about children, I have

---

some statements and questions that I hope will be a thinking ground for you.

"The child is laughing and smiling, they are not grieving."

Do adults not smile in the face of loss?

"The children are playing ("taking a break")...they are fine now."

Do adults not find ways to "take a break" from too much pressure or pain? Talking a walk, reading, journaling, eating, etc., are all ways that we use to free our minds for a brief period of time. As you incorporate the horse, notice what they do when they feel pressure...they move away.

"Children are too young to understand grief and loss."

Have you ever seen a young child taken from his or her mother or have you witnessed this rush of emotion from your own children? Think about how old they were and then ask yourself...are they really too young to grieve? I think that you will find the answer to be in their reaction.

"Don't tell her the truth about her mother dying, she won't understand."

Has someone ever told you something that was not true? Before you find out the real story, you create a million other scenarios in your mind...some of them worse than the truth. Children are no different. Their minds do work, just on a different level than ours. Take this example for instance. A mother is dying from cancer. Instead of taking time to explain to 5 year old Mary about her mother, you decide to tell Mary something YOU think that she will understand. "Your mother has a cold", you tell her. Later that week, Mary's mother dies. So every time someone gets a cold, what do

you think that Mary will think? It's the little things that mean the most. Taking time to explain the truth on their developmental level is one of the greatest means of support that can be given to children.

There are also three guidelines that I go by when addressing the needs of children in relation to a death, impending death or other type of loss. These help me remember to respect and validate children, no matter what their age. They are as follows:

Be honest, not graphic. Have you ever noticed how children will come back and ask you the same question over and over again? They want to make sure that you are telling them the truth. They need to trust you

to be honest with them, remembering honesty does not mean graphic details. After the terror attack of 9/11 on our country, I had the privilege of going to a preschool to be a counselor, or so I thought. Little did I know, I was the one who was going to be listening and learning. The children were already participating in their own form of therapy, reenactment. There were some who were holding invisible guns shouting "bang, bang...shoot the bad guys", some were coloring pictures of burning buildings, some were talking and laughing and some were just silent. They all knew what had happened and each had their own ways of expressing what they had been told and what they had seen. Use your own judgment but remember honesty does not need to contain graphic details. Simple facts will allow them to understand, without unnecessary clutter.

On their developmental level versus their chronological age. Most of us know children whose developmental level of understanding far exceeds their own chronological age. Always take this into account, no matter the age of the child, adolescent or teenager. This will also determine how they understand and process the death, impending death or loss. There is a possibility that a child will become "developmentally stuck." Even though the child gets older he or she can experience thoughts, feelings and even reactions that were experienced at the time of the death or loss, if subsequent deaths and losses occur. If you know this ahead of time, then it will be easier to assist them with these different and confusing behaviors.

With their own means of communication. Stories of loss are some of the most important stories that you will ever have the privilege of hearing.

Communicating the thoughts and feelings that convey the stories are just as important. Think about the ways in which you feel comfortable communicating. Children have their own ways as well. Don't assume that just because they are a young child that they will like to color or because they are a teenager that they will like to journal.

Be Ready! Have a variety of ways in which thoughts and feelings can be expressed, so that you don't miss the opportunity to hear the story that needs so much to be told and deserves so much to be heard.

Some examples of communication tools to have on hand are:
- Paper and markers, crayons and colored pencils
- Play dough, Model Magic or clay
- Paints, both finger paint and paints with brushes
- Stamps and stickers
- Glue
- Beads, yarn, ribbon
- Small and large craft boxes
- Books, both on the type of grief you are addressing and general interest ones such as a book on horses or cats or a funny story that has nothing at all to do with loss.

And the list will continue to grow as you put your tool bag together.

In addition to these guidelines, also become familiar with the role(s) that the children play in the family, both prior to and following the death. Some may have heard the phrases, "Little girls are to be seen and not heard" and "Big boys don't cry." Know that these suggestions can be taken to heart, especially when a child feels the family is counting on them. Think back to your experiences of death or times that you have been with other friends when there has been a death. It is not unusual for children to hear statements such as, "Now that your father is dead, you will have to be the man of the house" OR "Because your mother has died, it is up to you to take care of your dad." Can you imagine being the child that hears these words and the amount of imposed responsibility they must feel? As an adult, the reality of these situations can be overwhelming. For children they can be life altering and devastating.

There is also a term called *"magical thinking"* that refers to how children view aspects of death, dying and loss. Within this realm of understanding children blame themselves for what is happening or what has happened. Remember to be respectful and validating of their thoughts with this issue and avoid using statements such as, "There is no way that this is your fault...you are too young to cause this to happen anyway." Think how this would sound to you if you had been playing with your dad, had become angry because he had to go to work and said something like, "I hate you...I wish you were dead." Your dad doesn't come home because he was killed in a car accident. What would you think? In their minds the guilt and blame are real and need to be handled with care. Use examples of ways to show them that none of us have any control over our situations. One might be to have them sit with you and wish as hard as they can that it will snow while you both are sitting there. After a while it will be apparent that there is no amount of wishing in the world that would cause that to happen. Relate this to what is happening and gently redirect, not correct, their thoughts.

Another important idea to remember is that *a child's perception is their reality.* To diminish this by insisting that they are wrong in their thinking, can be very harmful. If the child is incorrect in their account of the loss, gently re-direct with open ended questions that allow them to feel safe and comfortable.

One more thought. Not all children will be saddened over the death. If there has been abuse, neglect, etc., there could almost be a sense of relief that you detect. Here is an incredible opportunity for you to validate the child's thoughts and feelings. There are many ways that you can do this, but one of the best ways is just to listen and be with them, as they work through adult issues within a child's mind.

We can all learn from children. Provide them with security and consistency within a supportive environment, where they can share their thoughts and feelings of grief and loss. Remember to validate and respect them by really hearing, not just listening, to all that they have to share. You never know, you might even learn something from their words of wisdom.

<chapter four>

Adults and Loss

AS we become adults, it is my opinion that we get caught up with "life." It is not by any fault of our own, but rather what comes with the responsibility of adulthood. We no longer are able to find the time to "just be" or are able to enjoy those memorable activities of our childhood such as skipping through a run away sprinkler on a hot summer day, with a glimpse of what used to be a bathing suit. Now, would that not turn some heads? Can you imagine the comments by your friends, family and neighbors?

Perhaps the horse lends us wisdom here. Have you ever watched a horse take a bolting run across a field on a brisk fall morning and then suddenly stop while the morning sun outlines their mane and tail blowing in the wind? Now that is living! They live instinctively with life, not analyzing whether it is the correct or acceptable way for them to act.

With grieving, it is no different. Somewhere we have learned that there has to be a right way to grieve and we have to follow a specific outline. Otherwise, it would not be done correctly and would not fit into the adult box. My question to this then is, *"What is the right way?" Do we become quiet and withdrawn? Do we stay so busy that we hope the memories will fade into the business of the day? Do we talk to people? Do we journal? How do we do it?*

My suggested answer to all of these questions coincides with a saying coined by a famous athletic company. We just do it..that's all. It is so important to know that the way one chooses to cope with their grief, if not self-destructive or harmful to others, is the way that is best for them. We have all been given a wonderful attribute from God called individuality. In that same manner, we all have individualism within the intricacies of the grieving process. Without it we would all think, act and grieve alike. Can you imagine how boring that would be?

As mentioned in Chapter 2, there is *healing in movement.* When working with adults support this idea by allowing them that same privilege of choosing a means of communication as we do with the children. In doing so you are providing a vehicle for movement that allows them to address their own individual grief in a manner that feels safe and comfortable for them. Providing this type of momentum creates a pathway for their healing to begin, still respecting and validating them as an individual.

Because we are adults we have also developed a phenomenal reasoning ability. Sometimes this reasoning can be used to one's own detriment as we slip into what I call the **should-a, would-a, could-a way of thinking.** In working with many adults who have experienced a death of someone they know, conversations will inevitably sound something like this. "I should have known he was getting ready to have a heart attack. I just thought it was his indigestion." "If only I would have watched her more closely...I just thought she was such a good swimmer that nothing could happen to her in that small pool." "This is all my fault. I could have stopped him from going out that night, but I was so tired of the fighting." Do any of these sound familiar?

Guilt, blame and shame are also big players in our reasoning abilities. Remember also the roles that they play in trauma from Chapter 2. Their importance with adults is not to be diminished, as all of these aspects of individualized grief are very real. It is important as a counselor NOT to dismiss anything that is of value to the person who is grieving. It may not seem reasonable to you, but remember, this is not your drama or your life.

Adults like children, need to take a break from their grief. Ask about their hobbies, things that are interesting to them and what they do for themselves. You will get more information about where that person is in regards to taking care of themselves, and their grieving process by being genuinely interested in who they are, without the death or impending death or even loss. For instance try the statement "tell me about some things you enjoy doing." If the person says, "There is nothing that I can think of doing since my husband died." There you go! A plethora of information, contained in one uncomplicated, but heart torn answer. Notice, from what she has told you that perhaps she is not able to see herself as an individual without her husband. There are multiple circumstances that could be the reason behind this comment. They were married for 40 years and she has been with no one else, he was controlling and did not allow her to think for herself, she was very dependent upon him for every decision, etc. Try to re-direct the focus back to her as an individual, remembering that "there is nothing" that she focuses on that would allow her some movement within her process. If you are doing EAP work, this might be an opportune time to introduce her to the horses. Watching each in their environment, discussing what they appear to be like in the herd and then discussing what they are actually like as individuals. Metaphorical relationships can be very useful at this time, asking which horse she thinks that she is most like and why, in an attempt to expose possible personality attributes that have been hidden, forgotten or lost since the death.

Sometimes you will also find that even though you are with adults, they still need your permission to be able to grieve, feel relief or to be content and even happy. As we spoke briefly in the beginning of this chapter, adults can lose their ability to *just be.* Think about it. If you are constantly taking care of others needs, others business, others schedules, others lives, do you really have time to focus on your own needs? So it is with those who are grieving. Many adults have families and responsibilities that make up who they are. They need you to say it is OK to take 30 minutes, a hour or whatever the time frame; to laugh, to cry or just to be in the moment not taking care of anyone but themselves.

Society also can dictate the way that we as adults feel we can or cannot grieve. Do you remember the gender sayings that some of us grew up with, as referred to in Chapter 3? "Little Girls are to be seen and not heard." And "Boys/Men don't cry." As trite as these sayings may seem, never underestimate the power and significance that they may hold for the adults that you are working with. If they have experienced a death at an earlier age, they may have residual concern from that experience. You may be able to recognize their uneasiness when they are recalling the death, by hearing their what ifs. Much like the should-a, would-a, could-a way of thinking, the what ifs also combine themselves with the magical thinking attributes of children discussed in Chapter Three. Thus, manifesting prolonged grief guilt and responsibility from their childhood adult life, for a death that they could not have prevented. Additionally, circumstances can suppress the expression of individual grief, even throughout adulthood. Again referring back to children who can become developmentally stuck with their grief, attempt to bring that information forward if you are working with an adult who has experienced the death of a parent, caregiver or sibling. There could possibly be unresolved grief issues that are preventing movement in any direction.

Some thoughts to remember as you are working with adults are:

- Their thoughts and feelings of grief and loss need to be validated.

- They may need your assistance to be able to recognize and utilize their own individual way of expression.

- They may need your permission to grieve or to be content.

- As with children, not all will be sad that the person has died.

‹ chapter five ›

All in the Family

In this chapter I am not going to go into depth about family systems theories. I encourage you to read, interview and listen to anyone who has extensive experience and knowledge about this unique group. The reading that follows, will address issues that I have had the privilege of learning from working with some of the families who have been a part of Mane Support. Notice I did call this group "unique", with the hope of not offending anyone. If you will take a minute to review the members of your family, I think that you will agree that they are unique in many ways. Thus the reason for my reference.

The most important piece of information that I can offer to you in regards to working with families, is first, never forget that they are all individuals and second, each of these individuals has an extended family branch. So metaphorically speaking, you could be addressing a forest of issues. Because they all come together to your sessions and because they have all experienced a loss, they do not all see it, feel it or react to it in the same manner. The more family members, the more intricacies of grief reactions you will need to be attuned to, as their thoughts and feelings begin to surface. For instance, I had the privilege of working with a family of 4 whose father/husband was killed in a tragic accident. It wasn't until we were into several sessions, did their individuality of their grief begin to emerge. The picture became very clear, as the oldest remained quiet, the middle became angry and the youngest showed his sadness. The mom stepped back and let her children go ahead of her. In fact, she did not attend the sessions for some time. Remember what was mentioned in Chapter 4 about giving adults permission to grieve. Case in point. She did not feel that her grief was as important as that of her children's, thereby denying herself any avenues for healing. Her healing began much later, after all of the children had grown older and had chosen their means of incorporating their father's death into their present lives.

For this family and others, open communication is one of the most difficult tasks for them to achieve. Whether or not a family has good communication skills prior to the death, remember they are now all individuals whose thoughts and feelings are very different. This can be so confusing for some families, who were a close knit unit. Now there is a missing spoke in their wheel which can create imbalance and uncertainty of direction. In fact it can go off into many different directions. On the other hand if communication skills were not in place before the death, you may see the family completely individualize or you may see them pull together to survive. In any case, the two of the most important things that you can do for families is to: *Listen and provide avenues in which they can see the obstacles that are in the way of their being able to communicate.*

Aside from seeing the family all together, it is helpful if I can also spend some time with each individual. This gives crucial information to them such as, do the children not want to cry and/or grieve in front of the parent because they are afraid they will upset them? Are the children taking on parental roles? Are the children concerned about who will be working to support them and is there enough money for food, shelter, etc? Is there an underlying turmoil of blame and/or resentment that is separating the family? Does the parent blame the children for the parent's death or do the children blame the parent for the parent's death? Does the parent have "secrets" about the death of the spouse that is causing tremendous pressure for them? Is the parent able to be honest about their feelings with the children? And the list could go on. As you can see having this valuable input in addition to what you are learning about the family as a whole, can give you a more complete arena in which to work.

While you are going through this process with families, also take time to observe one of your best resources, the herds (families) of horses. Notice that they have an established order of leadership, they are not afraid to be honest with issues that may arise, address them and come to a resolution; they have an incredible "life in the moment" attitude and have no problem in letting you know where you stand with them. Their honesty is simple and genuine. What a therapeutic model for families and for us as individuals!

⟨chapter six⟩

Understanding the Wisdom of the Equine Counselor

To understand the wisdom of the horse, one only has to spend time with them in their own environment. They have an incredible ability to mirror us and our emotions, to allow us to understand what it means to live in the moment, to be impeccably honest and to be present with their enormous measures of strength. It would be impossible for me to write all that you can learn from the horse and all that they can teach you about the participants you are working with and about yourself. Just like us, each is an individual and has different information to share. On the whole, what I can tell you is observe, observe and observe!!

As you pursue your work, remembering a large part of that work IS observing your equine counselors, it is important that you be versed in the physical aspects of the horse. Not to diminish the knowledge already gained with your experience or to be elementary in nature, but I would like to review, the basic anatomy of the horse...or at least the parts that we count on the most for communication. From head to hoof we see:

Ears

The ears have an uncanny ability to move independently. Can you imagine what it would be like to be able to hear both what was going on in front of you and what was going on behind you AND be able to process the events separately? What a gift! When observing or working with the horse, be aware of the way

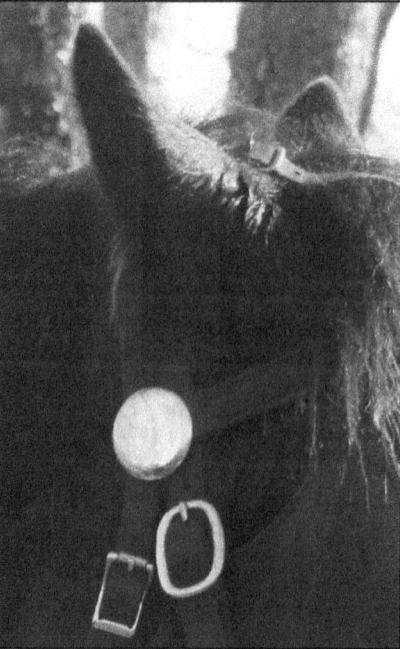

the ears are positioned. Are they telescoping all around? Is one ear pointed toward you and one toward the participant? Are they up or are they pinned? In my opinion, it is more important that you understand the meaning of the individual expressions of each horse in relation to this communication technique, rather than imposing suggestions of what ear positioning means onto the participant. By doing so, you will be more observant of the horse, its behaviors, while also maintaining safety for you and the participant.

Eyes

If the eyes are the window to the soul, then the horse has been gifted with magnificent bay windows that open wide to take in a full landscape. Unlike us, the horse has peripheral vision that reaches around to the hindquarters. They cannot see directly in front of them nor directly behind them, but their vision can encompass a wide perimeter of information.

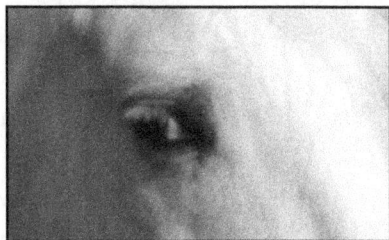

Nose

As soft and sensitive as the horse's nose is, one would think that you cannot touch it at all. However, if you have ever observed a horse on a cold morning (which I am sure that you have since observing is the best way to learn), you can watch them break a layer of ice off of the water to be able to get a drink. Now I ask you....what would that feel like to us if we broke ice with our nose? Yet on the other hand it can also serve as a communication tool, changing shapes with different smells or alerting the others in the herd of a possible danger with a single "blow."

Tail

If you have ever been "swished", you know that it is not the most pleasant feeling sensation, especially if your face happens to be in the direct line of fire. With a single swish, most horses are able to warn other herd members and/or humans of their frustration with a situation. In addition they can "flag" their tail to signal uncertainty, danger or excitement while taking flight. Let's not forget one of the most important uses for the tail, particularly in the summer, swatting flies.

Hoof

The hoof as a communication tool can be very powerful, especially when used as a means of defense or to express anger. There are other ways, however, that you can obtain information. For instance, placement of the hoof in relation to the participant's body,

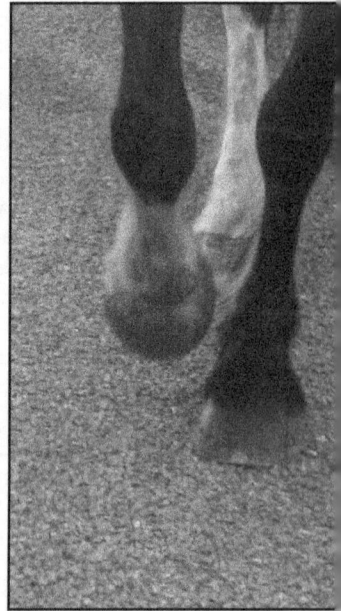

your body or another horse could be something important that you might want to notice. Is the client aware of any injury or pain? Do they respond if the horse steps on them? Does the horse consistently put their hoof back in the same place if they are moved away? In other words do they stand their ground, no matter what. Also notice if the horse is pawing at the ground with their hoof during a session. Could this action have perceived meaning to the participant or could this be a metaphor opportunity to continue the movement of healing? Are they bored? Are they challenging another horse? Are they frustrated? You can decide, but never underestimate the communication abilities of their hooves.

Neck

For those of you who have horses or who have been around horses, you know that another one of their most powerful, accepting attributes is their neck. If you have ever been one of the chosen ones who have had a physical "horse hug", you know that you have been granted one of the most powerful interactions possible. With tremendous strength in their neck,

they are able to channel their energy into a strong but gentle wrap of encompassing compassion. Remember how honest they are and then feel honored to be able to be accepted into their world.

Of course there are many other parts to the horse's anatomy. These are just a few of the ones that assist in focusing on possible reactions and/or interactions that could be catalysts for beneficial information.

Last but certainly not least, *take care of your horses*. Remember that they not only hear, but absorb intuitively and need time to "take a break" themselves…away from the all of the emotional input of humans. Let them play and be a horse, try not to schedule them back to back with participants and take the time to be aware of their needs. As an experiment, take the horse's heart rate and temperature prior to a session and then following. Record the actual physical responses that the horse is having, over a designated period of time. By doing so, you will gain more knowledge about your horse while assisting in minimizing possible stress related reactions for them.

The most valuable insight that I can offer to you is to take the time to watch, listen and learn from the wisdom of your equine counselors. Put yourself into their natural environment, interact with them and attempt to understand their distinctive and instinctive reactions. If they act differently with a participant or yourself, you will be able to more readily notice and perhaps gain more insight into the related circumstances or just be able to experience their healing power.

‹chapter seven›

Putting It All Together

N ow that you have some basic information and a better understanding of yourself, grief, trauma and the horse, consider the power that they all can have together.

First and foremost, it is my recommendation that you explore EAGALA, which was mentioned in Chapter One. Whether you want to start a business of your own, add to an existing business or just know more about the field of EAP (Equine Assisted Psychotherapy), this is the organization to learn from. Not only will you gain invaluable insight into the field, you also find support and opportunities for professional growth through certification, workshops and conferences.

After coming to a decision about what you want to do...take time to determine how you are going to do it. Develop a doable plan, using a SIMPLE approach. It is very easy, especially when you have a heart and passion for your work, to want to offer everything to everyone, during every minute of the day. Do a reality check for yourself. By taking the time to develop a solid foundation, you will be less likely to have to be concerned about the success later. In addition you will be taking care of yourself. Imagine having the time and energy for your program and having even more time and energy for YOU! What a novel idea!

As your program begins to take form, you may also want to think about the following:

- Is this going to be a private practice?
- Should it be a nonprofit or for profit? Remember to explore all of the pros and cons of each. There is much to be explored within each of these sectors.
- Develop a budget and determine the costs of all aspects of your program.
- Will there be a charge to participants and if so what will it be and will there be a sliding fee scale for those who cannot pay?
- Should you partner with another organization? Keep in mind your vision and align yourself with those you can trust and whose goals are similar.
- How are you going to market your program?
- Who will be supporting your program?

Once you have your program solid in your mind's eye, a suggested starting point is seeking out other individuals who are certified and who have the same passion for the work as you. I do not use the word "passion" casually. It is composed of many attributes that you also need to seek out in others that you work with...Honesty, Trust, Patience, Perseverance, and Flexibility, just to name a few. As a word of caution remember that you took valuable time in developing what and how you wanted your program to look like. Now also take that same "valuable time" in choosing someone to share your vision with. Be enthusiastic, yet patient. They will come, but be selective.

Determining the location(s), might be your next hurdle. It has been my experience that trying to accommodate everyone's travel needs, really did not affect the program. If people want to see you, they will find a way. After many long days of unnecessary concern about distance and location for participants, what I have found to be important is being in a place that is conducive to healing, safety and horses. Also if you are going to have more than one location, please understand that as much as you want to be, you cannot be in two places at once. This again goes back to being able to have confidence in those you have chosen to work with you. Develop a plan to ensure that your program's quality will be maintained and needs of the participants will be met, whether you are there or not.

The physical aspects now appear to be in place: program, staff and location. As you begin to review all that has been accomplished, step back, breathe and allow yourself to be basically flexible. Even though you may have it "just the way you want it", we all know what can happen to even the best laid plans. If some aspects of your mind's painting have just melted down the canvas, step back so you can see the whole picture. Think about the eyesight of the horse and take a peripheral view. Take a minute to remember why you started on this journey in the first place and know that it CAN happen!

The next area of development could be determining the population that you would like to work with. Even if there are several different ones, i.e., substance abuse, domestic violence, grief, etc., use the same methodical strategy as you did in the development of the overall program, location and staff. Attempt, once again, to paint a picture in your mind of who will be served when, where and how. Matching the experiences and knowledge of those you have chosen to work with you is a bonus here. For instance if you would like to do a group for widows and you have a staff person who has been a widow, use them. However, I would like to extend another word of caution here. Because you have done such a thorough job of understanding and selecting your staff, you will probably know this ahead of time. BUT...just in case...make sure that those you are utilizing for your groups and/or individual sessions have addressed their aversions and needs in their own journey of healing. There can be a transference of experiences that does not belong directly in the sessions with participants and that could cause more harm.

You now have in place, your solid vision for your program, location, staff and population(s) you are going to focus on, forget anything? The most important member of your team...your equine specialist!!!! Now its time to really do some work. Spend time focusing on this very important facet of your vision and get to know your horses or the horses you will be working with. Spend time with them, *just being.* Take time to review Chapter 6 and discover other parts of the horse's anatomy that are used as excellent communication tools. Again, one of the most important pieces of information that I can leave you with is to continually watch, listen and learn from the horses you are with. Their actions speak louder than our words.

There will be other intricacies that are specific to the type of program that you have decided to develop. Documentation will be your key to tracking your progress. A good rule of thumb to go by is, if it's not written it did not happen. Now it is up to you. If this is where you passion lies, the only way you will be disappointed is by not trying.

< chapter eight >

Last Minute Thoughts

BY being a part of EAGALA, I have learned many valuable tools. Some of which relate to grief work, which is my area of concentration, and some of which relate to me personally. Hopefully this guide has assisted in peaking your interest, to seek out what you need to pursue your vision and/or to continue your education in the field.

PUT THIS PLAN INTO ACTION. C.O.P.E.

C—*Seek* **Certification**
O—*Always* **Observe**
P—*Develop your* **Plan**
E—*Continually* **Educate**

Use all that you know and utilize it to its greatest potential, as you learn from the healing power of the horse.

Lastly, remember these thoughts:

Grief is a process, not an event. It does not have an ending point, but rather is defined as a continual, life changing journey.

The experiences of grief are as individual as we are. Each person grieves in their own way and time.

There is no right or wrong way for individuals to grieve. The exception to this statement comes with individuals expressing a desire to hurt themselves or others.

Watch out for the "should-a, could-a, would-a" trap. Review Chapter 4, realizing and being aware that this way of thinking happens to all of us.

An individual's perception of their situation, be it a child or an adult, is their reality. Reassure and/or redirect, if need be, with validation and compassion.

In as much as you give people permission to grieve, also give them permission to be happy. Remember that happiness can carry guilt for some who have experienced a death and they need to hear that it is alright for them to live and enjoy the life that is forever changed.

Children grieve too. Review the guidelines given in Chapter 3, Be Honest, On Their Developmental Level, With Their Own Means of Communication.

Spend time just being. In as much as you give this advice to the individuals that you work with, so you too need to put it into action.

Take the time to get to know your equine counselors. Whether you own the horse(s) or not, spend time in their environment with them. You might be surprised what you will learn about yourself.

Some of the most powerful words you will say to participants is " I don't know." As much as we would like to have all of the answers, the fact is that we can't. Also remember this process is about their decisions within their grief journey, not about our solutions for them.

Ask yourself this important question. **Why horses?** Now answer. They are wonderful to look at, but know the valuable information that they possess. Is it their uncanny ability to be so honest? Is it the mirror image that they provide us with? Is it their intuitive power that they come by so naturally, regardless of their size? Or is it their connection to our heart... *Hoof to heart.*

The following are recommended authors in the field of death and dying, equine behavior and well being and equine assisted psychotherapy. As with the book, this information is to get you started. There are many authors that may appeal more directly to what you are wanting to accomplish. Read, Explore and Question. This is how we learn, that in turn better prepares us to be able to hear the stories of others...whether through your own ears or through the spirit of the horse.

Recommended Authors

Grief and Loss

Charles A. Corr

Lynne Ann DeSpelder

Ken Doka

Linda Goldman

Robert Neimeyer

Therese Rando

Elizabeth Kubler-Ross

Catherine M. Sanders

Albert Lee Strickland

Alan Wolfelt

Equine Information, Care and Experiences

Tom Dorrance

Cherry Hill

Chris Irwin

Linda Kohanov

John Lyons

Kim Meeder

Pat Parelli

Sally Swift

Equine Assisted Psychotherapy/EAGALA
Lanier Cordell
Stephanie Dvorak
StarrLee Heady
Shannon Knapp
Mark Lytle
Randy and Patti Mandrell
Linn Thomas

Recommended Organizations
ADEC – Association for Death Education and Counseling
EAGALA – Equine Assisted Growth and Learning Association
TLC – The National Institute for Trauma and Loss in Children
American Academy of Bereavement
Parelli

<49>

references

References

Corr, Charles, A., Nabe, Clyde M. and Corr, Donna M. *Death and Dying Life and Living.* Wadsworth/Thomson Learning, 2003.

Doka, Kenneth J. *Disenfranchised Grief: Recognizing Hidden Sorrow.* Lexington Books, 1989.

Doka, Kenneth J. *Children Mourning, Mourning Children.* Routlege Taylor and Francis Group, 1995.

DeSpelder, Lynne Ann and Strickland, Albert Lee. *The Last Dance; Encountering Death and Dying.* McGraw Hill, 2002.

Steele, William. *The National Institute for Trauma and Loss in Children.* 2005.

www.ingramcontent.com/pod-product-compliance
Lightning Source LLC
Chambersburg PA
CBHW031525270326
41930CB00006B/528